SAFFRON & CURRANTS

A Cornish Heritage Cookbook
by Susan Pellowe

ISBN 0-9623507-2-9

Published by Renard Productions
100 N. Lincoln Way, Suite 2, N. Aurora, IL 60542 USA

Printed by United Graphics Incorporated
Mattoon, IL , USA

DEDICATION

To my father
William C. S. Pellowe
a Cornishman
who nurtured in me a deep affection
for that heritage

and to my mother
Lila Cook Pellowe
who baked and taught me to

Saffron refreshes the spirits, and is good against fainting fits and the palpitation of the heart. —Culpeper

"an herb of the sun and under the lion...which strengthens the heart exceedingly. ... Let not above 10 grains be given at one time, for the Sun which is the fountain of Light may dazzle the eyes and make them blind." —Culpeper

4

TABLE OF CONTENTS

INTRODUCTION

This booklet germinated one cold December afternoon in Mineral Point, a town in southwestern Wisconsin. This area was heavily settled by Cornish who came in the mid-19th century to mine the rich mineral deposits. As I browsed in the shop called The Cornish Miner, I found one of the most impressive collections of books about Cornwall that I had seen outside of Cornwall itself. The proprietor, Jim Jewell, and I fell into a meandering conversation. We learned we were both writers as well as enthusiasts for southwest England's farthest county. Combining those two interests, Jim had written a booklet about Cornish pasties. He asked whether I knew anything about saffron. Silly me, I admitted I did. He had had many inquiries about it, he said. If I were to gather my information about saffron in Cornwall and a few recipes...

The "gathering" has certainly expanded my information, not to mention my waistline. It has led to delightful correspondence, new friends, and new "old" recipes. I want to acknowledge especially:

Angela Broome of the Courtney Library, County Museum and Art Gallery in Truro, Cornwall, for addresses, recipes, and research into saffron fields;
Myra Burge, my sister, for her laughter and support;
The Cornwall Federation of Women's Institutes for permission to quote from Cornish Cooking, Ancient and Modern;
Rev. and Mrs. Derrick Greeves of Penrith, Cumbria: her Cornish roots, no doubt, sent her on the second mile in copying out saffron information and recipes for me;
Vida Heard, who so charmingly gave me permission to "use what you need" from her invaluable Cornish Cookery;
Jim Jewell, of The Cornish Miner;
Patricia Kimmell, an insatiable looker-upper, for references from her cookbook collection;
Bill Kitto, Mineral Point artist and former curator of Pendarvis, for permission to use his drawings and for Mineral Point lore;

Theodore Landon, for permission to use his etching "Since God
    Knows When";
Kori Oberle of Pendarvis historical reconstruction in Mineral Point
    for encouraging my association there and for permission
    to use the woodcut by Max Fernekes;
Jennifer Sharp, Mineral Point artist, for her drawing on the cover
    and the crocuses throughout the book;
Jim Simpson and the Tourist Information Council of Saffron Walden
    in England;
Bart and Fran Swindall for the use of their house in Mineral Point;
Ruth Tapper for information about Roman use of saffron in medi-
    cine and cooking;
Wendy and John Trewin for his being Cornish, for sharing their
    favorite recipe for Saffron Cake, and for letting me quote
    from John's two books of rich memories about growing
    up at the Lizard;
Countless friends who ate my test results.

Thank you all!!

Mineral Point is conscious of its Cornish heritage and has preserved
buildings and customs. Sites of special interest include The Gundry
House (Mineral Point Historical Society), the former gracious home
of a local merchant; Pendarvis, a complex of stone-and-wood workers' houses (Wisconsin State Historical Society), with special tours
and activities throughout the summer; Shakerag Street, a cluster of
older style buildings that has served as one of the centers for the
considerable colony of artists — several of national renown — who
make Mineral Point their home. Because of the combination of spe-
cially preserved Cornish heritage and the available artists, I have
chosen to illustrate this Cornish heritage book primarily with scenes
of Mineral Point by its artists.

These are the anchor buildings for the State Historical Society of Wisconsin restoration now known as Pendarvis, in Mineral Point, Wisconsin.

8

SAFFRON

The aroma would meet me at the corner of 9th Street and our alley. Wherever I meet it, it still takes me there.

I stand scuffling chestnuts or cinders as I watch my best friend go into her house across the street. Clutching my paper from school, I turn and slowly walk down the alley behind Lapeer Avenue in Port Huron, Michigan. My fingers bounce over dark bricks that are the back wall of the Methodist Church. Then: I smell it! I smile. I stop dawdling with bricks and I run, my golden sausage curls bouncing as I take the nearest route, a quick left beside the church to the narrow cement walk that diagonals across our big green yard. I pound through the always-unlocked back door, up the five steps and into the kitchen.

Saffron buns!

My mother is just taking another panful from the big oven, but the first ones are on the rack on the counter, yellow-orange, polka-dotted with currants or raisins, and cooled just enough for consumption. Standing near them sometimes is a bowlful of whitish butter my mother has just churned. Is it any wonder I am a chubby child?!

My Cornish father thinks Mother has baked these Cornish buns as a treat for him. I know she means them for me, too. I eat two or three — till she says, "Stop! You'll spoil your supper!" Who cares?! Who needs supper?? This is better than any supper. This is homemade saffron buns!!!

Have I ever tasted any as good, since my mother died? No, not even my own.

My dad cherished similar memories, except that the streets he used to run along were in Penryn and Flushing in Cornwall itself.

9

My mother had her childhood saffron memories, too — on a street in Laurium at the tippy-tippy-top of Michigan's upper peninsula.

Wherever the Cornish have migrated, they have taken saffron with them. In her *Cornish Cookery*, Vida Heard tells a true tale about saffron reaching Johannesburg in South Africa, where she lived for years, and where the police have apparently always been suspicious:

In the early days of Cousin Jack's emigration to the Rand mines, the nostrils of the Johannesburg Post Office sorters were assailed by certain letters from Cornwall, containing — what? On opening a letter for inspection, the police decided the bright yellow contents must be rank poison. In time, however, they realized their mistake and allowed the fragrant parcels through, in increasing numbers as the immigrants from Cornwall swarmed in.

THE PRICE OF IT!

Part of a Cornishman's working vocabulary is the phrase "as dear as saffron", meaning that something is terribly expensive. Every now and then, a friend in London tells me her friendly neighborhood grocer is not carrying saffron that year because the price has gone too high. In upscale specialty shops, one can pay as much as $6 or $7 per 1/32 oz. Buyer beware —that works out at $3072 to $3584 per pound! Our Illinois Cornish Society has found a source for LaMancha saffron that allows us to sell it for $10 per 1/4 oz. That varies by the year, depending on the crop, but works out to $640 per pound — still more than salt or cinnamon, but then one uses far less of it.

Why does it cost so much? Because its harvesting is labor intensive. To produce one pound requires approximately 75,000 hand-harvested stigmas plucked carefully from the centers of crocuses. Between the cost of labor, the need to work quickly when the crop is ripe, and the vagaries of weather (beating rains just at harvest may ruin the yield), there is sometimes a temptation to "pad" the product. Back in 15th century Nuremburg, they had very strict laws to ensure the purity of the product. Nevertheless, a few greedy merchants dared to adulterate their product by mixing it with other yellow plant substances. When the merchants were caught, they and their saffron were burnt at the stake.

10

When adulteration happens now, the procedure tends to be to sell the saffron already powdered and to add turmeric to it. Turmeric lends approximately the same color to food that saffron does, but of course not the same taste. In many African recipes where color rather than flavor is the purpose for adding saffron, I have seen lists of ingredients that read "saffron or turmeric". To a Cornishman, this is blasphemy! In certain markets, I am told — especially in the Far East — the blend of saffron and turmeric is accepted common practice. Beware if on your travels you think you're bringing home a bargain of saffron powder! Some markets also offer "saffron" that is actually dried safflower. Again, it adds color but not that unique flavor.

WHY IN CORNWALL?

How did this exotic and expensive spice become so popular in a remote and generally poor county at the west of England? It was not native there, although one can as readily as elsewhere cultivate a few crocuses for personal use.

Apparently a variety of influences introduced it. Cornwall for centuries mined and traded tin. Among the chief traders were Phoenicians from the east end of the Mediterranean. They seem to have known and used saffron, whether from contacts in India via Persia, or from Egypt, Greece, or Rome. Wherever they got it, the Phoenicians are credited by legend with first bringing saffron to Cornwall. We tend to forget how desirable spices used to be as trading commodities. With its diverse uses, saffron must have been one of the exotic and useful items the Cornish were willing to take in return for their metal. Further, the Phoenicians dedicated saffron cakes to the goddess Astarte, a mystique that may well have appealed to the Cornish.

The next likely influx came with the Romans who, together with the Greeks, were great consumers of saffron not only as a spice, but as a dye, a cosmetic, and a medicine. The Romans in Britain grew saffron in the gardens of their estates. We have some references to show that when they departed, monasteries — with rich land and free labor — continued to cultivate the bulbs and presumably to savour saffron in cooking. That came to an abrupt halt in 1536 with Henry VIII's dissolution of the monasteries. The King probably never foresaw that side effect, for he loved saffron.

Was saffron grown in Cornwall itself? As there were pockets suitable for vineyards — and vineyards are reappearing — were there fields suited to and vivid with blue-purple or deep yellow crocus? Again I turn to Vida Heard, who became intrigued with the question and spent considerable time tracking down records and traditions. She admits she was led up many a garden path with rumours of saffron parks and gardens, with tip-offs of saffron meadows at Gerrans and Feock.

She concludes that the Cornish use "saffron" as a generic color term in this sense and may call a field of yellow mustard or buttercups "a field of saffron." The Cornish are not alone in this. In Shakespeare's *All's Well that Ends Well*, Act IV Scene 5 opens, "No, no, no, your son was misled with a snipt-taffeta fellow there, whose villainous saffron would have made all the unbak'd and doughy youth of a nation in his colour." The usual explanatory footnote translates "saffron" simply as "yellow." *The Concise Encyclopedic Guide to Shakespeare* identifies saffron as "the color of cowards and jealous men."

But Vida Heard continues:
*In an article on Cornish Cooking in the **Cornish Year Book** (Bossiney 1982), that much-loved writer the late Marika Hanbury Tenison states with assurance:*
'For a long time the Cornish grew their own saffron, near and around Stratton, picking and grading the tiny stems of crocuses by hand.'
She gives no source of her information. But when I followed up her clue and wrote to Mr. Roy Thorn, Curator of Bude Museum, he replied to me as follows:

*'There is reference to the growing of saffron in a privately published book by a Mrs. C. Hawkey in 1871 titled **Neota** in which Mrs. Hawkey states '...while for culinary purposes there were to be found the angelica and caraway plants and the saffron crocus, within which blue petals was stored a supply of genuine saffron colouring for the manifold cakes and Revel buns for which Launcells was celebrated.'*

Launcells is a hamlet or parish adjoining Stratton, and the above account, explains Mr. Thorn, refers to Launcells' vicarage gardens.

Another indication of a true saffron field is given in a chapter of a book **Around the Fal** *published in 1983 by Extra Mural Studies, Exeter University. The author, Miss K N M Bowring, told me that she had met someone in the Mylor district who had known of a field at Penryn at the turn of the century that was actually sold as a saffron field, and was considered the last in production in Cornwall. As the field was owned by a medical man, she thought that the story has some credence.*

The Cornwall County Museum has tried to help track down evidence of saffron grown in Cornwall. Ms. Angela Broome of Courtney Library writes that the Cornwall Records Office has only this reference in their index so far (as of April 1989):
LEASE for 99 years dated 1 December 1653. John Treffry of Fowey to William Maior of Fowey, merchant.
re: SAFFRON MEADOW in Fowey.
LEASE for 99 years dated 9 December 1697. John Treffry of Place, Fowey, esq to John Pomeroy of Fowey, merchant.
re: SAFFRON MEADOW (as above).

In Cornish families, saffron buns are a treat that children don't forget and adults remember fondly. Every autobiographical reminiscence by a Cornishman that I have read includes a description of festivities in which saffron buns were for a while the center of attention.

Both Netti Pender and Douglas Tregenza, in writing of growing up in Mousehole, recall the Sunday School galas. They remember walking in procession behind a band to Chywoone to a field in front of someone's house. There amidst all the trappings of a big tea, they were given a big, traditional round saffron bun. Mr. Tregenza reports that some of them wrapped the buns in large red handkerchiefs to take home. A. L. Rowse also remembers at Sunday School teas enormous saffron buns "corrugated" with currants and lemon peel. Rowse tells too of his grandparents, who had a large family but very little money; their Christmas treat was a saffron cake, with a saffron bun and a cup of cocoa. One deduces that for some folks

13

saffron was an occasionally affordable luxury — something guarded and regarded as special, which nevertheless did not altogether break the bank.

Wherever the Cornish went, they kept their love of saffron. From the slate mines of Pennsylvania to the gold mines of Grass Valley, California, or Lead, South Dakota; from the copper and iron of Michigan and Montana to the silver of Mexico; in Australia and Cuba and South Africa, one finds little pockets where pasties and saffron buns are available.

None of this really answers "Why in Cornwall?" We have to settle for the answer that the Cornish liked saffron, they were willing to trade for it, it became traditional, and they kept it for the sake of the sausage-curled girls and long-legged boys who expected saffron buns as their due treat.

WHERE ELSE IN THE WORLD?

Historically, saffron's roots are royal and ancient. In the Song of Solomon in the Bible, it is listed among the chief spices: "Thy plants are an orchard of pomegranates, with pleasant fruits, camphire with spikenard, and saffron, calamus and cinnamon, with all trees of frankincense, myrrh, and aloes." (Chapter 4: 13-14)

Saffron joined cinnamon, frankincense, myrrh and cassia to perfume the oils that anointed the kings of Egypt. Cleopatra used saffron in some of her cosmetics.

According to legend, the crocodile is named for the *crocus sativus*, whose sweet fragrance caused him to shed his only tears.

Antiochus, a King in ancient Syria, employed 200 beautiful women to sprinkle the guests at his lavish parties with perfumes of cinnamon, lilies, and saffron. In Imperial Rome's wilder years, saffron not only was used to perfume the baths but was scattered through the Forum and was strewn before Nero when he entered the city. Talk about throwing your money around!

14

The Assyrians and Egyptians used it as a medicine 6000 years ago. The Romans used saffron as a flavoring, a dye, and a medicine. Apicius in his Roman Cookery Book calls for the flavor and color of three scruples of saffron in his recipe for vermouth. (A scruple is 1/24 ounce.) The other ingredients to be added to 18 pints of wine were an ounce of cleaned and pounded Pontian vermouth, one date (!), and six scruples each of mastic, costmary, and aromatic leaves like mint. Saffron was also part of his sauce for grilled lampreys — a very popular dish — along with pepper, lovage, savory, onion, stoned damson, wine, mulsum, vinegar, liquamen, defrutum, and oil. Saffron was also, according to Apicius, an item in aromatic salts.

It is prized as a stable dye. Supposedly in ancient Ireland saffron dyed a king's mantle. In India, shortly after Buddha's death, his priests made precious saffron the official color for their robes. In classical Rome, saffron was the traditional color for the bride's veil (*flammeum* = *flame-colored headscarf*) and shoes. By contrast, in ancient Greece saffron-colored garments were identified with the luxury of courtesans.

As a spice, it is used in northern European countries for festive breads such as Scandinavian St. Lucia buns and Estonian Christmas breads. In northern India too it is important in traditional holiday foods.

Long cultivated in Iran and in Kashmir's Happy Valley, it is thought to have been introduced to Cathay by the Mongol invasion. Almost recent history is its mention in Chinese medicine (*Pun tsaou*, 1582-68).

As Roman civilization died, Roman luxuries such as saffron faded from Europe including eastern England — if the tradition be true that the Romans had cultivated it there. For centuries it seems to have survived mainly on private estates. It remained popular in Africa, however, and the Moors re-introduced saffron to Europe when they conquered Spain. Spanish paella may be the dish that most Americans now associate with saffron, or perhaps its cousin Italian risotto. The French use it in bouillabaisse.

15

THROUGHOUT THE ISLE

A 10th century English leechbook (medical handbook) refers to saffron. In the 14th century cookbook *The Forme of Cury* — a collection of recipes compiled and used by master cooks to England's Richard II — half of the recipes called for saffron, so we know it had regained its popularity by then.

Legend has it that a lone traveler was responsible for re-introducing saffron "from Barbary to England." Hakluyt wrote in 1582:
It is reported in Saffron Walden that a pilgrim, purposing to do good to his country, stole a head of saffron and hid the same in his Palmer's staffe, which he had made hollow before of purpose, and so he brought this root into this realme, with venture of his life, for if he had been taken, by the law of the country from whence it came (thought to be Tripoli), he had died for the fact.

"Saffron Walden" means "saffron fields." The town of Saffron Walden is near Cambridge and is the site in Great Britain best known for its association with saffron. Amidst sheep and therefore wool, the town has for centuries been a weaving center. Saffron was valued as a dye applied to the distinctive white local cloth.

Although it is generally accepted that saffron fields were established here in Edward III's reign (1327-1377), the earliest actual record of *crocus sativus* in Saffron Walden is dated 1444-45, when it shows up as a commodity subject to tithing in an agreement between the Vicar of Walden and the Abbey of Walden. A modern publication from the town's Tourist Information Council tells that in 1481 one Geoffrey Symonds of Heyreman left by will two houses, two saffron gardens, and a field to pay a priest for performing services, and in the same year in the Churchwarden's Accounts we read that there was trouble when pigs broke into saffron gardens and did much damage — a repeated offense.

The first detailed description of its local cultivation comes from the writings by Rev. William Harrison in his *Description of England in Holinshed's Chronicles*. He recounts early rising so
(continued on page 39)

ᴪᴪᴪ

TENDER SAFFRON SCONES

3 cups sifted flour
2 teaspoons baking powder
1/2 cup sugar
1 teaspoon salt
3/4 cup butter or oleo
1/2 cup (or more) currants or raisins
1 egg, well beaten
milk — almost a cupful
1/4 teaspoon crumbled/ground saffron

Place 1/2 cup milk in a small heavy saucepan; add saffron and heat almost to scalding. Quickly remove from heat and let steep for 30 minutes.

Sift together flour, baking powder, sugar, and salt. With knives or a pastry cutter, cut the cold butter or margarine into dry ingredients until the mixture is the consistency of fine crumbs. Add currants or raisins. Beat the egg in a one-cup measuring cup; fill it to the 3/4 cup mark with the saffron milk, using additional plain milk if necessary. Stir lightly into dry ingredients. Add a bit more milk if necessary to make a soft dough. Turn onto lightly floured board or waxed paper; knead lightly. Roll out to 1/2 inch thickness. Cut into rounds.
Place on lightly greased baking sheet. Brush tops with a little extra milk and sprinkle with sugar.
Bake at 400 degrees for 10-12 minutes, until golden.
Serve with clotted cream and marmalade or jam.
Yield: about 20 scones.

ᴪᴪᴪ

MOTHER'S SAFFRON BREAD AND BUNS

Our neighbors at our cottage on Lake Huron were Rev. and Mrs. Chapman. He had come from St. Neot in Cornwall, and as young men he and my dad helped each other build summer cottages side by side — places that became the one permanent home that these Methodist ministers had.

Even in the primitive stove-top ovens they afforded for their cottages in those days — which in fact approximated Cornish cloam ovens more than today's appliances do — Mrs. Chapman and my mother managed to turn out breads and pies. The only recipe for saffron bread that I have found in my mother's index-card recipe file is labeled "Mrs. Chapman's Saffron Bread," so I am left to assume that this is the recipe Mother used and that I loved. It works for me now and I still love it.

> 1/2 Tablespoon sugar
> 6 Tablespoons lukewarm water
> 1-1/2 packets dry yeast
> 7-1/2 cups flour
> another 1/2 Tablespoon sugar
> 1/4 cup warm water
> 1 cup shortening
> 1 cup sugar
> 1 Tablespoon salt
> 1/2 teaspoon ground saffron
> 1/2 cup warm water
> 1 cup currants
> 1 cup candied fruit peel and/or almonds, raisins, or
>   just more currants

Crumble or grind the saffron; pour over it one cup boiling water and leave it to steep for an hour.

In a medium bowl, mix 6 Tablespoons lukewarm water and 1/2 Tablespoon sugar; sprinkle over it 1-1/2 packets of dry YEAST. Leave it for 10 minutes while it feeds on itself and bubbles. Stir gently if necessary to be sure all yeast is working.
When it is bubbly, slowly stir in 1-1/4 cups warm water, 1/2 Tablespoon sugar, and 2-1/2 cups flour. Cover with a plate and put in a warm place until doubled and spongy — about 45 to 60 minutes.

In a large bowl, cut the cup of shortening into the cup of sugar mixed with 5 cups of flour and the tablespoon of salt. Add the currants and fruit, mixing so fruit is nicely floured. When the first batter is doubled and bubbly, pour it into this bowl of flour, along with the saffron water. Stir and add more warm water if needed (maybe 1/4 to 1/2 cup) to make a nice soft dough. Turn onto a floured board and knead until smooth. Return dough to bowl; cover; set in warm place to rise until double in bulk.

Punch down dough. Shape it into bread or buns and let rise again for about an hour until double in bulk.

Brush with milk. Bake at 350 degrees.
Buns should bake 20-25 minutes, round loaves on a baking sheet should bake about 25 minutes; small loaves take 30-35 minutes and large loaves 35-40 minutes. Mrs. Chapman says that this makes 3 large loaves or 3 dozen buns, but I always mix 'n' match! — and get one large loaf, 1-1/2 dozen buns or more, and one or two small round loaves for gifts.

WENDY'S SAFFRON CAKE

Most cookbooks warn us to use saffron sparingly. Poppycock. True, used sparingly saffron has a delicate flavor – a few strands scattered over a custard sauce add a pleasant finishing touch for the eye the nose, the palate. True, too, that one probably wants to proceed cautiously in identifying the strength of flavor most satisfying to individual taste. But I vote with John Trewin's sentiment that most saffron cake today is pale. I like the generous application of saffron in this recipe that his wife, Wendy, makes for his birthday. Here indeed are the great golden buns he writes of. A delicacy, yes! But delicate? No! Hearty enough for a proper schoolboy treat and so rich that it's no wonder the Cornish don't bother to serve them with butter. It is important to know that **"cake" here means a rich bread**; do not expect a dessert pastry with frosting.

> 1/64 oz. saffron (.5 gram) in 1/2 cup boiling water
> 1 packet regular dry yeast
> 1/2 cup milk
> 1 teaspoon sugar
> 4 cups all-purpose flour
> 1/4 cup sugar
> pinch of salt
> 1/2 lb. butter (or half lard or shortening or oleo)
> 1 oz. candied fruit peel (or more, to taste)
> 1/2 lb. dried currants

Grind the saffron to a note-too-fine powder and steep in the 1/2 cup boiling water overnight (6 hours or more).
In a small bowl, mix the 1 teaspoon sugar with the 1/2 cup warm milk; sprinkle the yeast on top and let dissolve and bubble; you may need to stir to be sure all yeast is dissolved.
In a large bowl, cut together flour, sugar, salt, butter; stir in the peel and currants.

When the yeast rises, pour it and the saffron water into the flour mix and stir to make a soft stiff dough. You do not need to knead this dough, but stirring and turning it with a wooden spoon will accomplish the same thing.

Cover bowl with a large plate andput in warm place to rise.
Grease your pans and when the dough has doubled in bulk, shape
it into loaves or buns, put into the pans, and let rise again.
Bake at 350 degrees for 50-60 minutes.
This will make 3 small loaves or 1 large loaf (9 x 5 x 3) and 9
medium buns baked in an 8" square pan.

As with any popular food, "best" recipes are handed down, ring-
ing minor changes on the basic formula – insisting on all butter,
all lard, half-and-half, etcetera; more or less flour in proportion;
spices or not; eggs or not. The Women's Institute cookbook includes ten recipes for saffron cake! They all include currants and
9 of 10 specify dried fruits (our mix of cherries, citron, lemon and
orange rind is not the same, but it is tasty). The amount of saffron called for varies and the method of measuring, from "6d
worth" (sixpence) to tincture of saffron.

W.u.Kitto   Polperro

SAFFRON SPLITS

Cornish Splits may be described as a yeast-leavened scone and therefore often slightly drier than others. These are heavenly served warm or, the next day, split through horizontally, toasted, and buttered. They have quite a strong saffron flavor and a warm, reassuring aroma.

3/4 cup milk
1/4 teaspoon ground saffron
2 Tablespoons sugar
1 packet dry yeast
1/4 cup lukewarm water
3-1/2 cups all purpose flour
1 teaspoon salt
2 large eggs, beaten
1/4 cup dried currants
(optional: 1/4 cup dried candied peel)
2 more Tablespoons milk

With mortar and pestle, grind saffron threads to medium-fine. Put them into a small heavy pan; use the 3/4 cup milk to rinse out the mortar and capture all the saffron, emptying it into the pan. Scald, then cool.

In a small bowl or a measuring cup, mix just 1 teaspoon sugar with the lukewarm water; sprinkle the yeast over the top and leave to dissolve and bubble (about 10 minutes).

Sift together in a 3-quart bowl 3 cups of the flour, the remaining sugar, and the salt. Make a well in the center of the flour. Into this pour the cooled milk, the beaten eggs, and the frothy yeast mixture. Blend. It will be stiff-ish but still sticky.

Put about 1/3 cup flour onto a board. Turn the dough onto the board and knead, adding more flour if necessary. Knead until dough is smooth and no longer sticks to the board. Put dough back into the bowl and set a plate on top. Let sit in a warm place until doubled in size (about an hour).

(An unlighted gas oven with just the pilot light to keep it at about 100 degrees is perfect.)

When doubled, punch down. (Flour your hands as needed; literally punch your fist into the center of the risen dough, then use your hands like a rubber spatula to swoop dough from edge of bowl to center. It will deflate.)
Turn onto lightly floured board and gently knead in the currants (and dried fruits if used). Let the dough rest while you grease well a heavy baking sheet. Break off pieces of dough the size of one to two large eggs. Place 1-1/2 inches apart on sheet. Brush lightly with the 2 Tablespoons of milk.

Bake at 375 degrees ion preheated oven for 15 minutes — until golden and firm to the touch.
Remove to racks to cool.
Yield: about 18 splits.

Note: instead of shaping into buns, this may be shaped into a loaf and baked in a well-greased 4-1/2 x 8-3/4 inch loaf pan for 20-25 minutes.

SAFFRON SPREAD ON
FRENCH BREAD

Soft butter
Ground saffron
Loaf of French bread

Cream butter with ground saffron to taste — I like 1/8 teaspoon ground saffron to 1/2 cup butter, which generously slathers one loaf.

Cut the bread diagonally, cutting down *to* the bottom crust but not *through* it (same technique as for garlic bread). Spread the butter on both sides of each "slice". Wrap the loaf in foil and place in 400-degree oven for about 12 minutes, until heated through. Serve hot. This is especially good with bouillabaisse.

SAFFRON TEA BREAD FIT FOR A KING

This is on the order of a pound cake. It melts in the mouth when fresh from the oven, but the flavor is even better after the bread has stood for a day or two.

- 2 cups flour
- 2 teaspoons baking powder
- 1 teaspoon salt
- 1/2 cup shortening
- 1/4 teaspoon baking soda
- 1/4 teaspoon crumbled/ground saffron
- 1/4 cup hot water
- 1/2 teaspoon grated lemon rind
- 3/4 cup sugar
- 2 large eggs
- 1/2 cup water
- 2 Tablespoons lemon juice
- 1/2 cup dried currants

With mortar and pestle, grind saffron fine; empty it into a cup; add the 1/4 cup hot water and allow to steep for 30 minutes.

Sift together flour, baking powder, salt; set aside.
In a large bowl, blend the shortening, soda, and grated lemon rind, taking care that they are well mixed. Beat in the sugar. Beat in eggs, one at a time. Combine lemon juice with the 1/2 cup water; use this to rinse the remaining saffron powder from the mortar and pestle; add this and the saffron water to the batter alternately with the flour, beginning and ending with the flour.
Beat with electric mixer for half a minute.
Stir in currants.

Grease and flour two 7 x 3 x 2 inch loaf pans. Divide the batter between them.
Bake at 350 degrees for about 50 minutes, until the top is golden and a toothpick inserted into the center comes out clean.

Cool in pan about 10 minutes before carefully removing. Finish cooling on cake rack.

Serve alone or with butter, cream cheese, or clotted cream. Store airtight in a cool place.

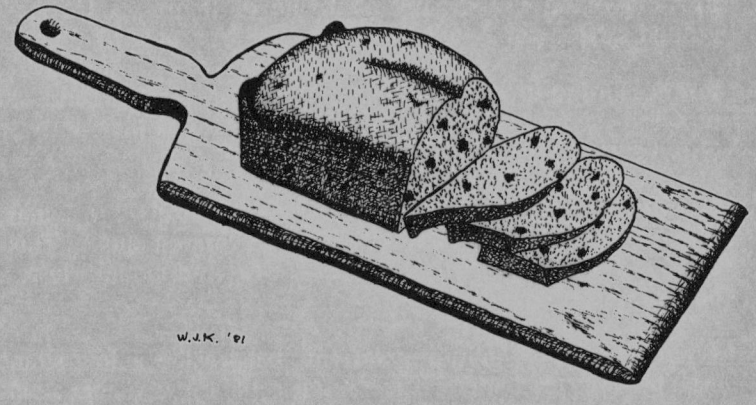

W.J.K. '81

This drawing of a loaf of currant-laden saffron tea bread originally appeared on artist Bill (and wife Evie) Kitto's Christmas card in 1981 — and the bread was handcolored with a dye steeped from Spanish saffron. Inside the card he printed this note about a special custom in Mineral Point, Wisconsin:

"A cherished custom of Cornish households was to have freshly baked "Christmas Saffron Cake" to share with friends and neighbors during the holiday season. Partaking of a slice of cake from a neighbor's house traditionally assured one of good fortune for a month. Consequently, much visiting back and forth resulted, as all sought to sample twelve varieties of this exotic treat, thereby anticipating a full year of happiness."

25

Use sparingly. Too much tastes bitter, "medicinal". Experiment and write down how much you use until you discover what is best to your taste. However, see note to Wendy's Saffron Cake.

For Coloring, use 1/4 teaspoon in 2 Tablespoons of hot water. This will prettily color 5 to 6 cups of flour.

For Flavoring breads, my own rule of thumb is 1/4 teaspoon ground saffron for 2 to 3 cups of flour. You may like less.

For seasoning in sauces: 1/8 to 1/4 teaspoon of ground saffron in 2 Tablespoons of hot water or white wine will pleasantly season 6 to 8 servings (about 2 cups).

For bouillabaisse or other stew-type dishes, use 1/2 to 1 teaspoon ground saffron to eight cups of liquid ingredients. This is a generalization, subject of course to individual taste and pocketbook.

When powdering/grinding saffron, keep aside a few strands to crumble into the batter. The presence of a few visible strands in the finished product proclaims that this is a genuine article.

Dried saffron has a long shelf life. Archaeologists found that saffron discovered in Egyptian tombs had retained its properties and was still usable! Stored in a dry place away from light or excessive heat, 2 to 4 years is a reasonable expectation. Some cooks recommend "renewing" it before use by placing it in waxed paper on a sheet in a low-temp oven until paper begins to curl and brown -- they say this lowers its acridity.

Methods of adding saffron to ingredients vary. No single method is "right". It may be beaten into the shortening or butter, with or without first powdering it. It may be crumbled into a liquid and allowed to infuse. It may be ground fine and then covered with boiling water to steep. (One recipe calls for

"The Lizard means for me... the hot spicy tingle of saffr usually a wretched substitute, a pale, dry affair, meagre thick with currants, a cake like a great gold sun. They sa

steeping it for two days!) You may choose whatever is convenient. Steeping allows greater release of flavor and color. Always hold back a little liquid from your recipe and use this to rinse the steeping container, in order not to lose any of that precious gold.

In today's kitchen, saffron uses include breads, tea cakes, rice, veal, chicken, soups, sauces, bouillabaisse.

Measuring saffron. Saffron is sold by grains, drams, grams, ounces, 1/16 oz., 1/32 oz., .2 or .5 grams -- all very confusing. That is why in this book amounts are often translated to portion of teaspoons. As a buying guide:

    1 dram = 1/16 oz.   (.0625 oz.)
                (26 grains -- not threads-- equal 1 dram)
    1 gram = 1/32 oz.   (.0352 oz.) = 1/2 dram
    .5 grams = 1/64 oz. (.0176 oz.)
    .2 grams =   (.007 oz.)

The 1/2 dram is a common measure in old recipes.
I usually figure that 1/2 dram will yield me 1 generous teaspoon powdered saffron, or 2 teaspoons crumbled saffron. Therefore 1/64 oz. (a common measure to find in the spice section of stores) will yield 1/2 teaspoon powdered or 1 teaspoon crumbled.

Where to buy saffron and for how much. Look for it in the spice section of your grocery store; if it is not there, ask your grocer whether he can order it for you, or whether he keeps it behind the counter (some store it in the safe!). Try ethnic grocers, especially Indian, Spanish, Mexican. You can order by mail from Ivey's Pharmacy, High Street, Mineral Point, Wisconsin 56535, and from specialty mail order food shops that advertise in cooking magazines. The 1/64 or 1/32 oz. Containers in 1998 cost under $5. If you plan to have fun experimenting, you'll realize what a savings it is to find a supplier by the ounce (1998, $30-$60). Split it with a friend — and give them a copy of this cookbook! — and you can each play to your heart's content.

cake in the ovens of Kynance Bay. Saffron cake now is without character when it should be moist and spiced and is an acquired taste; rather it is a taste to be acquired."
--J. C. Trewin in *Up from the Lizard*

What made the English people sprightly was the liberal use of saffron in their broths and sweetmeats.

—Sir Francis Bacon,
who used a concoction of it to preserve life

CHICKEN IN MILK AND HONEY

This recipe dates from the time of King Richard II. I used to serve it at medieval-style dinners, as it is easy to make in quantity and it holds well for serving buffet style.

> 1 3-to-4 pound chicken, cut into serving pieces
> 1/2 cup flour, mixed with salt and pepper to taste
> 3 Tablespoons cooking oil
> 3 cups milk
> 1/3 cup honey
> 3 Tablespoons minced fresh parsley
> 2 small leaves fresh sage, minced (or 1/4 teaspoon of
>   ground sage)
> 1 teaspoon hyssop, ground (mint leaves are the handi-
>   est and most common modern substitute)
> 1/2 teaspoon ground savory
> 1/4 to 1/2 teaspoon saffron, ground
> 1/8 teaspoon freshly ground pepper
> 1/2 teaspoon salt
> 1/3 cup slivered almonds
> rice

Dredge chicken in flour mixture. Brown it in oil in a heavy pan until it is golden on both sides.
In bowl, combine milk, honey, and herbs. Pour this well-mixed liquid over the browned chicken, stirring to combine drippings with the sauce. Cover. Simmer for about 30 minutes, until meat is tender. Just before serving, stir in almonds.
Serve over rice.
Serves 4.

CURRANT TEA BREAD

1 cup cold tea
1/2 cup dried currants
1 teaspoon baking soda
2 cups sifted all-purpose flour
2 teaspoons baking powder
6 Tablespoons sugar
6 Tablespoons shortening

In a saucepan, bring the currants and tea to a boil. Cover and simmer for 5 minutes. Remove from heat, stir in soda, and leave to cool. In a mixing bowl, mix together the flour, baking powder and sugar. Cut in the shortening so that the mixture becomes the texture of breadcrumbs. Add the cooled tea and currants. Stir to mix well.

Pour into two small loaf pans (7 x 3 x 2 inch) that have been well greased. Bake at 375 degrees for 35 minutes or until a toothpick inserted in the middle comes out clean. Cool for a few minutes in the pans, then remove to a rack.

This may also be baked as one large loaf (9 x 5 x 3 inches); allow 45 minutes baking time.
Instead of currants or along with them, try cut-up apricots, raisins, or semi-dried figs, or 3/4 cup mixed candied peel. The fruit takes on some of the flavor of the tea and of course the bread does, too, so choose the flavor of your tea accordingly and experiment creatively. For instance, apricot tea with apricots. Darjeeling is a good general tea flavor. Even a generic tea bag brewed to medium strength is nice.
Good fresh, this renews wonderfully when toasted and served with butter and jelly!
Makes one or two loaves.

NEGUS

1 Tablespoon black currant jam
boiling water

Put the jam in the bottom of a mug. Fill the mug with boiling water and stir well. This is said to be a good drink for sore throats.

CURRANY 'OBBIN

This and the Figgy Hobbin that follow are traditional oldies and must be considered together. The paragraph-format recipes come from the Women's Institute cookbook. Like the Hevva Cake which follows, it is basically pie crust.

Make a stiffish paste with flour and lard and a pinch of salt, not no baking-powder. Wet it up with milk if you got it, and water if you ab'n got it. Roll it out nice and thick and sprinkle it all over with currans, nice and thick. Then roll it up careful like you would your starch clothes, squeeze home the ends and brush it over with the white of an egg if you want it to shine. Then clap 'en in the ob'n. The children do dearly like it, and as they say currans be full of they new-fangled "vitamines" the Doctors be always ordering, they ought to be good for 'em.
P.S.—If you tired of currans you can make a "figgy" wan fer a change.
P.P.S.—Figs is just Cornish for raisins.

FIGGIE HOBBIN or FIGGIE DUFF

Take a little suet, a little lard, teaspoonful baking-powder, rub this into 1/2 lb. flour, add figs* to taste. Mix with cold milk or water to a stiff paste. Roll into 4-inch squares about 1/2 inch thick. Cut across the top and bake 1/2 hour. *Sometimes called figgy duff. A notice was seen in a shop window not long since, "Figgy Duff, 4d lb. More Figgier, 5d."

An Updated Version:

> 2 oz. lard
> 2 cups flour
> 1/2 teaspoon salt
> 1/3 cup currants
> cold water

Cut the lard into the flour and salt. Gradually add enough cold water to form a malleable dough — about 1/4 cup. Knead lightly. Roll out to 1/8 inch thick. Scatter with currants or "figs". Fold the bottom third up and bring the top third down over it and seal lightly by pressing together. Slash the top with a knife. Brush with milk. Bake at 350 for about 30 minutes.

I found that if I truly rolled this like laundry, I had too many layers that did not bake through!

ᙡᙡᙡᙡᙡᙡᙡᙡᙡᙡᙡᙡᙡᙡᙡᙡᙡᙡᙡᙡᙡᙡᙡᙡᙡᙡᙡᙡᙡᙡ

In *The Winter's Tale*, IV iii 38-52, the Clown studies his shopping list:

> *Let me see, what am I to buy for our sheep-shearing feast?*
> *Three pounds of sugar, five pounds of currants, rice... I must have saffron to colour the warden pies; mace; dates—; nutmegs, seven; a race or two of ginger, but that I may beg; four pounds of prunes, and as many of raisins o' the' sun.*

(Warden pies were made of winter pears; a 'race' of ginger is a 'root' of ginger.)

ᙡᙡᙡᙡᙡᙡᙡᙡᙡᙡᙡᙡᙡᙡᙡᙡᙡᙡᙡᙡᙡᙡᙡᙡᙡᙡᙡᙡᙡᙡ

HEVVA CAKE
The Fast-Food Dessert!

Among Cornish fisherfolk this was a celebration treat that could be put together in a hurry by the wives when they heard the men bring their boats in loaded with a good catch and shouting "Hevva! Hevva!" ("Heavy! Heavy!") It does not mean that the cake is heavy! Nor is it exactly what we now think of as a cake. "Cake" is a general term here for a "sweet." I suspect it was created as a portable currant pie, because it is really just glorified pie crust with oodles of currants baked throughout a single thick layer instead of between two thin layers. What would you call it?! — it's not a cookie nor a pie, so "cake" is as good a term as any.

Notice that the ingredients are simply what the cook has on hand. Like the "Currany 'Obbin", different recipes differ. One calls for all lard, another for all butter; some call for milk as the liquid, some for water, for cream or even clotted cream. Some add an egg or a bit of lemon peel, some 1/4 or 1/2 teaspoon of "spice" — often nutmeg and cinnamon. Some add a little candied fruit peel along with the currants.

Treat this as a basic recipe, then, and like our forebears vary it according to what you have in the cupboard.

> 3 cups flour
> 2 ounces butter
> 2 ounces lard
> 1/4 teaspoon salt
> 1 Tablespoon sugar
> 1 cup dried currants
> 3/4 cup milk

Put in a bowl the flour, butter, lard, salt and sugar and cut together until butter and lard are small crumbs. Add the currants, then stir in the milk.
As you take it from the bowl, shape it into a ball with your hands. On a floured board, roll it into a circle 1/4 to 1/2 inch thick

(NO THICKER, OR IT WILL NOT BAKE PROPERLY). Lift onto a greased baking sheet. With a sharp knife, cut nearly through the dough to form wedges — like cutting a pie into pieces. This will help it break apart when you remove it from the oven. Brush with a little milk and bake at 400 degrees for 30 minutes.

Cool on a rack.
This recipe makes two rounds about 8 inches in diameter, which will cut into 8 wedges each.
If before baking you sprinkle them with sugar, they make a good breakfast pastry.

Another method of making Hevva Cake seems akin to making croissants. Here is a version of that, with typical instructions:

1 lb. flour	6 ounces currants
1 lb. fresh butter	pinch of salt

Take 1/4 lb. butter and rub into the flour, make it into a stiff dough with cold water; having added the currants and salt, roll it out on the board, take another 1/4 lb. butter and lay it in small pieces over the dough, flour and fold it up, roll again twice, adding the remainder of the butter, then roll it out finally an inch thick; score the surface in small diamonds, brush over with milk and bake for half an hour in a quick oven.
(From Mithian W. I.)

RED CURRANT SAUCE

1 teaspoon butter, clarified
2 Tablespoons lemon juice
1/2 cup red currant jelly

Warm the butter in a heavy pan. Slowly stir in the lemon juice. Add the jelly and stir with a whisk over low heat until all is blended. Adjust to taste.

To serve, pour over individual serving of ham, duckling, pheasant, or goose.

PORTER CAKE

A full-flavored non-sweet tea bread, Porter Cake keeps well if wrapped tight and stored cool. But why keep it? Wrap up a couple of thick slices, put them in a sack, add a teabag, stop by a friend's and enjoy an instant surprise party!

> 1/4 lb. butter
> 3/4 cup sugar
> 1 egg, well beaten
> 1/2 cup porter (stout) at room temperature
> 2 cups all-purpose flour
> 1-1/2 cups currants
> 1/4 teaspoon mixed spice (allspice, cinnamon, nutmeg, cloves)
> 1/2 teaspoon baking soda

In a heavy 2-quart pan, melt the butter over low heat; do not allow to brown. Remove from heat.
Stir in the sugar, then the beaten egg and the porter.

In a separate bowl, combine flour and currants. (I also like to add a little candied dried mixed peel, although that is not strictly traditional.) Stir the mixed spice into this and add to the batter in the pan. Stir well. Last, sprinkle the soda over the batter and mix well for several minutes.

Spoon into a well-greased and floured 9 x 5 x 3 inch loaf pan.
Bake at 350 degrees for about 90 minutes. It will be medium brown and smell divine. Test with a toothpick to be sure it is baked through. Cool for a few minutes in the pan, then turn onto a cake rack to cool. While it cools, cover it lightly with tinfoil or a doubled cloth to keep it from drying out — otherwise the crust may rip when you cut it.

TO WHET THE APPETITE FOR STILL MORE...

Finally, a few very distinctive Cornish dishes have not been mentioned because they lie outside the realms of saffron and currants. However I am sure there will be discontented readers if this "Cornish Heritage Cookbook" ignores these:

Cornish Fairings are cookies — flat, crispy, spicy rounds in which ginger dominates. (The English do love ginger, from chocolate-covered candied ginger to ginger beer. Gingerbread is also very popular in Cornwall.) Fairings could be baked at home, but they were also sold by street vendors and at fairs — hence, apparently, their name.

Mahogany is a drink supposed to keep the fishermen going in all weathers. Interpret that as you will when you read the ingredients: 2 parts gin to one part treacle (molasses), well beaten.

Pasties (pronounced PASS-tees), like tacos or pita pockets or sandwiches, are a hand-held meal — an essential take-along for miners or farmers or fishermen. For poor people in bad times, pasties contained only potatoes and onions, or palatable weeds or offal — always it is proper to use whatever is at hand. As a dessert, they may hold fruit. Rumor says that some clever cooks put a division inside the pasty, with the main course in one end and dessert in the other! Historically, early pasties were made with barley flour. Now a common recipe for crust uses an egg as part of the liquid, which gives a firmer product than the recipe that follows here.
There is also a difference of opinion whether the pasty should be crimped around the edge, or whether ingredients should be placed in the center of the dough circle and the two sides brought together and crimped along a center line over the top.
Recently I have seen a new product in supermarkets, called a Foldover Meat Pie — which is just a pasty called by a name that people can pronounce without hesitation.

For lots more lore about pasties, see Jim Jewell's excellent *It's Time for Pasty!*

References from that invaluable *Cornish Recipes* provide endless delight. Of **Black Cake** (a fruit cake with almond paste and icing), it tells "This recipe has been used in a Cornish family for many generations. Several cakes are made from above ingredients; one is always kept twelve months and eaten on its birthday, when the new batch is made for the coming year." From St. Mawgan it gives the "Ingredients for a **Great Cake**" that would be great indeed: "5 lbs. butter brought to a cream, 5 lbs. flour, 3 lbs. white sugar, 7 lbs. currants, 2/6 worth perfume, peel of 2 oranges, pint of canary [wine], 1/2 pint rosewater, 43 eggs (half ye whites), 1 lb. citron." For a **Squab Pie** from Penzance it is the instructions that startle; after layering 4 lbs. of meat and a cormorant in "a large pie-dish", the cook is to "Cut up half a dozen apples very thin, also half a dozen onions; mix and proceed to ram apples and onions into every conceivable crevice....Bake for 1 or 1-1/2 hours, or longer should the pie be very large or the cormorant very tough."

Remedies. For Hoarseness: rub the soles of the feet before the fire with garlic and lard well beaten together. **For Constipation:** as a last resource, eat boiled currants. **For Sciatica.** carry a nutmeg in your hip pocket, or a potato until it withers, and the sciatica will be cured. [from 1929]

Seedy Cakes are a white loaf cake with caraway seeds mixed in. My grandmother's recipe calls for

> 3 full cups flour
> 1 cup sugar
> 1-1/2 cups lard and butter mixed
> good pinch of salt
> 1 full Tablespoon caraway seeds
> 2 teaspoons baking powder
> 2 or 3 eggs or a little milk

That's the order she listed them in. My method is:

Cream together the lard, butter, and sugar. Beat in 1 cup of flour sifted together with salt and baking powder. Beat in the eggs, add seeds, then the remaining flour.

Put into two 7 x 3 x 2 inch buttered-and-floured pans. Bake at 350 degrees for about 45 minutes, until a toothpick inserted in center comes out clean and top is golden. Cool on rack and slice.

ππππππππππππππππππππππππππππππππππππππππππππππ

THE PELLOWE PASTY

Savoured any time, but unfailingly served as Christmas Eve supper in our family. Warning: this is not a sturdy traditional crust to be carried around. It is light and flaky.

CRUST

> 3 cups all-purpose flour
> 1 cup shortening
> a little salt
> about 1/3 cup cold water

Cut together flour, salt, and shortening until crumbly. Stir in water a little at a time to make a soft dough. Turn onto waxed paper and knead briefly till smooth. Cut the ball into quarters; roll each into a circle.

METHOD

On half the circle, place layers of whatever ingredients you fancy. Common items for ours are (all raw):

> potatoes sliced about 1/4 inch thick
> round steak cut to strips an inch or two long
> onions, chopped
> carrots sliced into "pennies"
> small cubes of rutabaga (swedes, the English call them)

Per person, allow 1/4 pound meat, one medium potato, half a small onion, and 1/4 cup or so of whatever vegetables you choose. We always keep the cut-up vegetables in bowls of water; as we take a handful, the clinging water keeps the pasty moist.

Season with salt and pepper. Sprinkle on a little crushed or ground thyme or marjoram. Dot with butter.

Fold the other half over this and crimp the crust around the outer edge. Make knife-gashes in the top to form the initial of the person whose it will be. Brush with milk. Place on baking sheet. Bake at 350 degrees for 45 minutes.

Makes 4 or 5 pasties.

ππππππππππππππππππππππππππππππππππππππππππππ

Soups. Saffron Soup, a gourmet specialty, simply adds up to 1/4 teaspoon ground saffron to 5 cups of common potato soup made with potato, onions, and milk. For centuries Cornish cooking depended on whatever simple foods came from garden and wayside, stretched with water. For **Kiddley Broth** (Kettle Broth), the cook put bread (probably leftover barley bread) into a bowl, then poured in the liquid from boiled onion, adding butter, pepper, and salt to taste as well as a few marigold heads if available. An even poorer soup was **Gerty Gray:** a little flour and a lot of water boiled together.

Starry-Gazy Pie's history is a cousin to Hevva Cake. One Christmas about 200 years ago, the fishing village of Mousehole, near Penzance, was threatened with starvation. Crops were poor and the weather so stormy that ships had not been able to leave harbor. Tom Bawcock — desperate, brave, and determined — rounded up a crew willing to brave the storms. Against the odds, they returned safely and loaded down with seven kinds of fish. The date was December 23. Ever since then, the village of Mousehole has celebrated Christmas Eve's eve as Tom Bawcock's Eve. The traditional meal is this fish pie made with seven kinds of fish and a sturdy crust, constructed with fish heads emerging from the crust to gaze at the stars.

OLD DOLLY PENTREATH'S COTTAGE, AND THE KEIGWIN ARMS (15TH CENTURY) MOUSEHOLE

(Continued from page 16)
that crokers (crocus growers were called "crokers") might finish picking by 11:00 a.m., before blossoms would wilt. He says that 30,000 large stigmas would yield 5 pounds of wet saffron, which dried down to one pound. Harrison calls for "warme nightes, sweet dews, fat grounds and misty mornings." (Contrast that count to today's 75,000 stigmas to one pound of dried saffron. Were their stigmas that much larger than today's, or were dyeing needs less rigorous than cooking needs? In fact, stigmas-per-pound depend on the crop, its maturity, moisture level, amount of base still attached.)

Today the town's purple-and-yellow heritage is preserved in decor and in officialdom. Eight saffron flowers are carved on one of the arches of the south aisle of the town's magnificent church, itself a symbol of Tudor prosperity. On the Charter to the town from Henry VIII, five *crocus sativus* blossoms appear on the arms of the Corporation. They are also on the mace from 1685. The crocus appears on the town's coat of arms and in plaster decorations on old cottages.

Henry VIII loved saffron so much that he considered women using it as a hair dye to be wasteful and he forbade their doing it. Up to the reign of King George III, royalty visiting England were presented with a silver salver "filled" with saffron. A veritable King's ransom?

In London, the gardens of Ely Place grew quantities of saffron. Saffron Hill is still on the map, running parallel to Farringdon Road from Clerkenwell to Charterhouse; it stops just by the church. There is also a Saffron Close in NW11, just off Finchley Road at Bridge Lane, not far from a Carmelite convent. This proximity to churches seems a significant reminder of its medieval associations.

How does all of this relate to Cornwall? During all those centuries of saffron's cultivation in England, tiny Cornwall is reported to have consumed approximately 20% of all that was produced. That's a lot of treats!

ΨΨΨΨΨΨΨΨΨΨΨΨΨΨΨΨΨΨΨΨΨΨΨΨΨΨΨΨΨΨΨΨΨΨΨΨΨΨ

STRICTLY FOR MEDICINAL PURPOSES

Although most writings about saffron include the phrase "often used for medicinal purposes," the reference nowadays remains general and vague. Finding specific formulae for remedies using saffron as an ingredient requires dedicated sleuthing in ancient sources and in books on herbal medicine. It used to be that the pharmacy was where one bought saffron — a vestige of its earlier usage. Some pharmacies still carry it, but, like Ivey's Pharmacy in Mineral Point, Wisconsin, merely as a convenience to their customers. Pharmacists today do not include saffron among their medical ingredients and they warn against any attempt to use it to treat any condition.

In the past, general references gave saffron credit for curing — or at least alleviating — such a variety of ailments as jaundice, gout, rheumatism, seasickness, coughs from consumption, fever, plague, and indigestion. Vida Heard gives this recipe from Cassell's *Dictionary of Cooking* (1896) for relief of indigestion:
Add a pinch of saffron to a quarter of a pint of hot water, then infuse for 10 minutes. Stir in two or three tablespoons of brandy (or any other spirits) and add a lump of sugar. Serve hot or cold.
She comments, however, that the alcohol probably has more effect than the saffron!

On the one hand we read that bees — who of course drink it neat — become intoxicated in saffron crocus fields; on the other hand, the Romans believed saffron "allayed the fumes of wine and prevented drunkenness."

Paracelsus, a physician of the 16th century, included saffron in many of his medicines. He claimed it relieved pain and inflammation from gout and he prescribed it for rheumatism.

Other common uses were as a diuretic (to eliminate water) and as a sudorific (to cause sweating). It was used to encourage measles and scarlet fever to break out so that the patient could begin recovery.

Because it was thought to aid blood circulation, it was used as an anti-inflammatory remedy against arthritis. It was said to encourage easier menstruation, but was therefore not to be used by pregnant women lest an inadvertent overdose cause hemorrhaging. Large doses were believed toxic. Some herbalists agreed that by itself saffron had little effect but that it acted as a catalyst for the other herbs and spices with which it was combined.

It was believed to help restore tissue and to be rejuvenating. One legend about its powers comes from India, where because of its reputed beneficial effects on circulation saffron is often part of a most powerful formula for rejuvenation, Chyavanprath. The concoction is named for the elderly sage Chyavan. The blindfolded daughter of the Emperor came to the woods where Chyavan was performing his rites. Not knowing who he was, she ran her fingers through his hair. Her father the Emperor came into the scene, saw this behavior, and ordered the sage to marry the girl, for it was improper for a woman in India to touch more than one man in her life. Chyavan agreed to marry on condition that the wedding be delayed for two months. During that time, he prescribed for himself the potion now named for him. It so rejuvenated him that he was able to give the girl marital happiness! (Chyavanprath is based on gooseberry concentrate, high in vitamin C.)

There is a recipe for a "saffron tea remedy", an infusion of a very few grains of saffron in boiling water. I'm afraid it reminds me of Vida Heard's comment about saffron in alcohol — but this time it is the hot water that is beneficial.

BOTANICALLY SPEAKING

Botanically, saffron comes from *crocus sativus*, a hardy dwarf member of the crocus family popularly called The Saffron Crocus. The name "saffron" seems to be an adaptation of *za'faran*, the Arabic word for *yellow*. It is native to southern and central Europe, the Levant, and western Asia. Most crocuses bloom in spring, but crocus sativus blooms in the autumn.

41

A classic description of the plant comes from the famous medieval herbalist John Gerard in 1597:

'The floure doth first rise out of the ground nakedly in September, and the long small grasse leaves shortly after the floure, never bearing floure and leafe at once. The which to express, I thought it convenient to set downe two figures before you, with this description, viz., The root is small, round, and bulbous. The floure consisteth of six small blew leaves tending to purple, having in the middle many small yellow strings or threds; among which are two, three, or more thicke chives of a fierie colour somewhat reddish, of a strong smell when they be dried, which doth stuffe and trouble the head. The first picture setteth forth the plant when it beareth floures, and the other expresseth nothing but leaves.'
[These refer to drawings in his book.]

HARVESTING HEAPS OF PURPLE

Most saffron today is grown in Spain, Italy, and India. The variations in product are slight. The Italian is said to be more pungent than the Spanish. Leading chefs warn that the Indian is most likely to be diluted or "contaminated" and therefore cheaper because not pure.

The hot flat area of Mancha in Spain — yes, Don Quixote country! — sets the standard for saffron. For two weeks, hundreds of farmers and townspeople abandon all else while they harvest saffron. From sun-up until about noon (by then the flowers wilt in the hot sun), they pick the vivid purple blossoms that have bloomed that morning and toss them into large baskets slung around their necks. The baskets are sent to the growers' houses, where women mostly but a few men too carefully and quickly pluck the bright orange-yellow stigmas from the blossom center, letting the "used" flower drop to the floor. After a few hours, the workers may be sitting knee-deep in fragrant purple! Each person's daily production is carefully weighed. Part of their pay is that they are allotted 1/4 of their output to take home. They may use some of it, sell some, hoard some for future private sale.

Baskets of harvested crocus blossoms ready for plucking.

The wet threads are roasted carefully over charcoal or wood fires, where they shrink and deepen color to a rich yellow-red. (Brown saffron is over-dried.) Five pounds of wet saffron typically roast down to one pound. Some growers pride themselves on quality control in that their workers do not retain the tiny bulb at the end of the stigma, which adds nothing but weight to the final product.

If you want to grow a little of your own saffron as an exercise in patience, plant the corms (bulb-like) in mellow soil in the spring. (In Saffron Walden, the crokers chose land with chalky soil — a temperate dry clay on a substratum of chalk.) Allow the plant to "ripen" fully or it will perish.

Harvest it when it blooms in the fall. Pluck the three yellow-orange stigmas from the center of each blossom. Dry them by spreading loosely on a large sheet and placing them in a low-temperature oven. This will hardly duplicate Mancha's best, but it will unquestionably prove a conversation piece.

You might like to consider this advice given growers in 1698:
> *Saffron is a great Improver of Land, and will grow in indifferent good Ground where it is not Stony nor too Wet, and in this case having Ploughed your Ground in to Ridglands, as for Corn or Pease, teake your Roots (a Bushell of which will set an Acre), and having drawn a Drill with a large Hoe, place them therein with the Spurns downwards, about three inches asunder; then draw another Drill, so that the mold of it may cover up the former, and in that place others in the same manner, and successively, till you have set your Roots, and when they Spring up, draw Earth about them, and these you must set in the beginning of July, and if the Weather be exceeding dry, you may sometimes water the top ranges, and in September the Blew Flower appears, and in it upon opening, three or four Blades of Saffron, which you must observe to gather out Morning and Evening for a Month together, the Flowers continually increasing.*
>
> *The saffron being gathered, you must make a Kiln, about half the bigness of a Bee Hive, of Clay and Sticks, and so putting a gentle Fire of Charcoal under it, tend it by often turning, till you have reduced three pound of wet Saffron to one of dry; and on this case the one Acre of Saffron will amount to the value of between Forty and Fifty Pounds in Money, the two Crops, for the Roots will yield effectually no more, without being renewed or transplanted, and thus much for the improvement of Land, by these profitable means and methods.*

CURRANTS

Currants are a popular ingredient in cooking from Land's End to John o' Groats, which means they are not viewed as a regional specialty so much as saffron is. I personally associate them with Cornwall, however, again because of my Cornish father. He always loved a few currants in his sugar cookies, and I loved them too, because Mother rolled out the cookies, cut them into rounds, and used the currants for eyes, nose, and mouth.

Dad also liked currants sometimes in oatmeal, and used to ask for them in apple pie. Apple pie?! I did think that was peculiar — until my first visit to Cornwall. There, in bakeshop windows and tea rooms and homes, I saw and ate apple pies with currants. That was when I began to understand where my father's preferences came from and what it means to have Cornish roots!

I remember my cozy happiness too when I bought my first saffron bun in Cornwall. It was in Falmouth at a bakery along the Parade. The bun was yellow and huge and packed with currants. The woman at the counter put it in a little paper bag just big enough to hold one bun. I carried it reverently. I grinned all over my insides as I chose a special place by the waterfront to sit while I ate my golden treasure. I held it carefully over the open bag in order to catch any currants that fell. After I finished the bun, I emptied a dozen currants from the bag into the palm of my hand and had them for dessert!

The history of currants is not nearly so complex as that of saffron, although it does have its own little surprise: currants are named for the Greek city of Corinth!

The original corinth is a raisin or dried fruit from a dwarf seedless variety of grape native to the eastern end of the Mediterranean. Hence they were called "corinths" or "raisins of Corinth." The word "currant" is a corruption of that.

It was probably the 16th century when shrubs of the genus *Ribes* were first imported from northern Europe to England. They bore small round red or black berries. They are cousins of the gooseberry and at first they were called "beyond the sea gooseberry." Lyte, a 16th century herbalist, called them "Bastard Currants." Through common mis-use, they became known as currants, red or black. Although the distinction is dying out, some people in England still refer to "shop currants" or "grocer currants" to mean corinths. The fruit from the *Ribes* — which one can pick from the garden without the grocer as middleman — they call simply "dried currants" or once in a while "dried gooseberry currants." I'm not sure what they would get if they were to refer to "bastard currants." Strange looks, probably.

CURRANT USAGE

There are just a few recipes here for currants. I trust you can figure out all sorts of uses for currants on your own. As I've suggested, they work wonderfully as faces on sugar cookies and a great pseudo-Jack-o'-lantern for Halloween. They are equally at home on flat gingerbread cookies. Knead them into bread, especially saffron bread. Sprinkle 1/2 cup into an apple pie. Stir currants into hot cereals. Toss them into cooked rice, pasta salads, rice pudding, tapioca, oatmeal cookies, hot cross buns, pumpkin bread ... wherever one might "normally" think of using raisins. Take your cue from what is so aptly called Pitchy Cake in the Women's Institute cookbook:
Take some dough of bread after it has risen and work in (i.e., "pitch" in) some goodness (fat), currants and sugar. Let it rise again for a short time and bake.
They do make a pleasant change — smaller, slightly more tart, a more concentrated flavor, not quite so sugary. They are a good source of vitamin C.

Currants in Cornwall are used in both meat and dessert pies. A Goose Giblet Pie calls for them, as do an Eel Pie and a Curlew Pie. A recipe for Duck Pye (from the Women's Institute cookbook) is worth quoting in its entirety — not so much for the currant usage as for its "starting from scratch" in a way few of us today have to:

46

DUCK PYE

Make a puff paste crust, take a couple of ducks, scald them, and make them very clean, cut off the feet, the pinions, the neck and head, all clean picked and scalded, with the gizzards, livers and hearts; pick out all the fat of the insides, lay a crust all over the dish, season the ducks with pepper and salt, inside and out, lay them in your dish, and the giblets at each end seasoned; put in as much water as will almost fill the pye, lay on the crust, and bake it, but not too much.
(Dated 1753, from the St. Stephens W.I.)

Besides Currant Pie itself, the most common dessert pie with currants is Mince Pie — which that invaluable Women's Institute book again tells us used to be oblong in shape at Christmastime, to imitate the manger where Jesus was laid. Currants are almost invariably present too in boiled puddings; the example we know best is Plum Pudding.

Black currant or red currant jams or jellies are tasty not only on toast, but in thumbprint cookies, in peanut butter sandwiches, decoratively dolloped into the middle of a dainty dish of rice pudding, or spread on pancakes. Traditionally, red currant jelly is served with pheasant, sometimes with duck or venison, occasionally with goose (after all, currants are a form of gooseberry....)

A red currant sauce is nice with ham. Often in old Cornish recipes for meat stews or casseroles, we find a couple of Tablespoons of red currant jelly and a glass of wine stirred in during the last half hour of cooking time. Best of all, I love black currant jam or jelly spooned onto a heap of Cornish clotted cream that has been slathered onto a scone made with what else but currants!

Extremely popular throughout Britain is Ribena, a black-currant juice drink sold as concentrate or ready to drink in bottles or boxes. The black currant flavoured syrup used in usually alcoholic drinks and in desserts is cassis, or *creme de cassis*, from the French.

47

Currants are almost never eaten uncooked. But you can buy fresh currants — if you want to make your own jelly, for instance — at some good produce counters or at farmers' markets. Ask for them. In the northern US, they ripen during July. And yes, besides red and black, they do legitimately come in white.

Dried currants are available all year. Look for them in grocery stores near the raisins and other dried fruits.

In Mineral Point there are several historic hotels and restaurants that proclaim on their signboards, "Since 1836" or "Since 1834", Evan's Eatery was an old ice cream shop that erected this sign, with a figure of a miner above, just as artist Theodore Landon shows and spells it!

Since God Knows When   *Theodore Landon*

BIBLIOGRAPHY AND FURTHER READING

Day, Avanelle and Lille Stuckey, **The Spice Cookbook**. Illustrations by Jo Spier. New York: David White Co., 1964.

Fitzgibbon, Theodora. **A Taste of the West Country**. London: Pan Books, 1975.

Flower, Barbara and Elisabeth Alfoldi-Rosenbaum, Editors and Translators. **The Roman Cookery Book by Apicius** (A Critical Translation). London: George G. Harrap & Co., Ltd., 1958.

Frawley, Dr. David and Dr. Vasant Lad. **The Yoga of Herbs**. Santa Fe: Lotus Press, 1987.

Hayes, Elizabeth S. **Spices and Herbs, Lore and Cookery**. New York: Dover Publications, 1980.

Heard, Vida. **Cornish Cookery: Recipes of Today and Yesteryear**. Trewolsta, Trewirgie, Cornwall: Dyllansow Truran, 1984.

Hemphill, Rosemary. **Penguin Book of Herbs and Spices**. Harmondsworth, England: Penguin Books, 1966.

Jewell, Jim. **Time for Pasty!** Mineral Point, Wisconsin: The Cornish Miner, 1985.

Martin, Edith, Editor of First Edition in 1929. **Cornish Recipes Ancient and Modern**. Truro, Cornwall: 21st Edition, 1962.

Pasco, Ann. **Cornish Recipes Old and New**. Penryn, Cornwall: Tor Mark Press, 1988.

Pender, Nettie M. **Mousehole: History and Recollections**. Mousehole: J. J. Pender, 1977.

Rombauer, Irma S. and Marion Rombauer Becker. **The Joy of Cooking**. Indianapolis: Bobbs-Merrill Company, Inc., 1975.

Szita, Ellen. **Wild About Saffron, A Contemporary Guide to an Ancient Spice**. Day City, CA: Saffron Rose, 1987.

Tierra, Michael. **Planetary Herbology**. Santa Fe: Lotus Press, 1988.

Tighe, Eileen, Editor. **Woman's Day Encyclopedia of Cooking**, Volume 10. New York: Fawcett Publications, 1966.

Tourist Information Center Publications, Market Square, Saffron Walden, England.

Tregenza, Douglas. **Departed Days: Mousehole Remembered**. Redruth, Cornwall: Dyllansow Truran, 1984.

Trewin, J. C. **Down to the Lion.** London: Carroll & Nicholson, 1952.

——. **Up from the Lizard.** London: Carroll and Nicholson, 1948. Reprinted as Number One in The Cornish Library by Anthony Mott, Ltd., London, 1982.

Ward, Diane Raines. "Saffron: Versatile Spice, Ludicrous Price." *Smithsonian*, August 1988, 104-110.

Seal from The Borough of Saffron Walden

Ͷ൯Ͷ൯Ͷ൯Ͷ൯Ͷ൯Ͷ൯Ͷ൯Ͷ൯Ͷ൯Ͷ൯Ͷ൯Ͷ൯Ͷ൯Ͷ൯Ͷ൯Ͷ൯Ͷ

> *Hail, many-colored messenger, that ne'er*
> *Dost disobey the wife of Jupiter;*
> *Who with thy saffron wings upon my flowers*
> *Diffusest honey-drops, refreshing showers....*
> —Ceres in Shakespeare's
> The Tempest, Act IV Scene 1, line 78

Ͷ൯Ͷ൯Ͷ൯Ͷ൯Ͷ൯Ͷ൯Ͷ൯Ͷ൯Ͷ൯Ͷ൯Ͷ൯Ͷ൯Ͷ൯Ͷ൯Ͷ൯Ͷ൯Ͷ

A Conversion chart for
SAFFRON & CURRANTS:
A Cornish Heritage Cookbook

Measurements in this book are given in American terms. Use this chart of equivalents to translate to British and metric measurements. Bear in mind that equivalents are approximate, not exact.

AMERICAN	IMPERIAL/METRIC

Dry Ingredients

Sugar:	I Tablespoon	I Tablespoon/15g
	1 cup	8 oz/240g

Flour:	1 Tablespoon	1/4 oz/7g
	1/4 cup (4 Tbsp)	1 oz/30g
	1/2 cup	2 oz/60g
	1 cup	4 oz/115g

Baking soda:	1 teaspoon	1 teaspoon/3g
Baking powder:	1 teaspoon	1 teaspoon/3g

(3 teaspoons = 1 Tablespoon = 7g)

Butter/Oleomargarine/Lard/Vegetable shortening

2 Tablespoon	1oz/30g
1/4 cup (4 Tbspns)	2 oz/56g
1/2 cup	1/4 lb/110g
1 cup	8 oz/225g

Currants/Dried Fruit/Candied Fruit Peel

3 cups	1 lb/.5kilo

Liquid Ingredients

1 Tablespoon	1/2 fluid oz/14ml
2-1/2 cups	1 pint/.5l

(Note: the US cup contains 8 oz/236ml/16Tbsp/48tsp; the Imperial cup contains 10oz/284ml/20Tbsp/60tsp)

<u>Yeast</u>
In the US, one cake of compressed yeast =
        1 Tablespoon active dry yeast
One packet of dry yeast = 1/4oz = 7g = 2 tsp
1-1/2 packets dry yeast = 1 Tbsp

OVEN TEMPERATURES

AMERICAN (Fahrenheit)	BRITISH (Celsius)	(Gas Mark)
250	130	1/2
275	140	1
300	150	2
325	170	3
350	180	4
375	190	5
400	200	6
425	220	7
450	230	8
475	240	9
500	250	10